SUPER ETENDARD

Series Editor : Christopher Chant

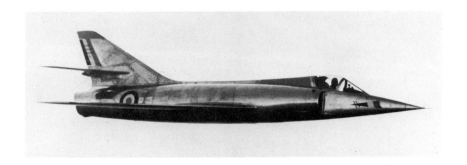

Foulis

Haynes

Titles in the *Super Profile* series:

Boeing 707

B-29 Superfortress

Harrier

Sea King

Super Etendard

F-4 Phantom II

ISBN 0 85429 378 7

Further titles in this series will be published at
regular intervals. For information on new titles
please contact your bookseller or write to the
publisher

© 1983 Winchmore Publishing Services Limited
First published 1983

A FOULIS Aircraft Book

Published by:
Haynes Publishing Group
Sparkford,
Yeovil,
Somerset BA22 7JJ

Distributed in North America by:
Haynes Publications Inc.
861 Lawrence Drive,
Newbury Park,
California 91320, USA

Produced by:
Winchmore Publishing Services Limited,
40 Triton Square,
London, NW1 3HG

Picture research Jonathan Moore
Printed in Hong Kong by Lee Fung Asco Limited.

Contents

Genesis   8

Development   15

Etendard IVM into Super Etendard   31

Action in the South Atlantic   45

Operational Assessment   52

The Future   53

Specifications   54

The first prototype of the Dassault-
Breguet Super Etendard shows off its
clean lines.

The air war in the South Atlantic in the spring of 1982 dramatically demonstrated the destructive potential of first-division modern weapon systems. British Sea Harrier FRS. Mk 1 and Harrier GR. Mk 3s armed with AIM-9L Sidewinder missiles proved deadly in air-to-air combat, beating theoretically faster aircraft. But it was the combination of the Super Etendard naval strike fighter and air-launched Exocet AM.39 anti-ship missile that was recognised as perhaps the greatest danger to the British surface fleet.

The success of Harrier/Sidewinder and Super Etendard/Exocet shows how important is the combination of weapon system and weapon platform — that is, the capability of the missile and the capabilities of the aircraft or ship which carries it. The subsonic Harrier shot down supersonic Mirages while the

Super Etendard, itself barely capable of Mach 1, used the advanced capabilities of the AM.39 plus its own sophisticated avionics to make long range stand-off attacks against warships and confound any attempts at interception. If the weapon platform was not shot down first, the weapon system was virtually unstoppable.

In fact the Harrier, Mirage and Super Etendard, although very modern aircraft, trace their design ancestry back a long way. The Harrier goes back to the P.1127 VTOL prototype of 1961, the delta wing Mirage first flew in 1956 while the Super Etendard is an extensive rework of the original Etendard IVM designed in the early 'fifties and first flown in 1956.

Carrying an AM.39 Exocet missile and sporting the insignia of 11 Flotille on its fin, Super Etendard no. 6 races down the flight-deck of the carrier *Clémenceau*.

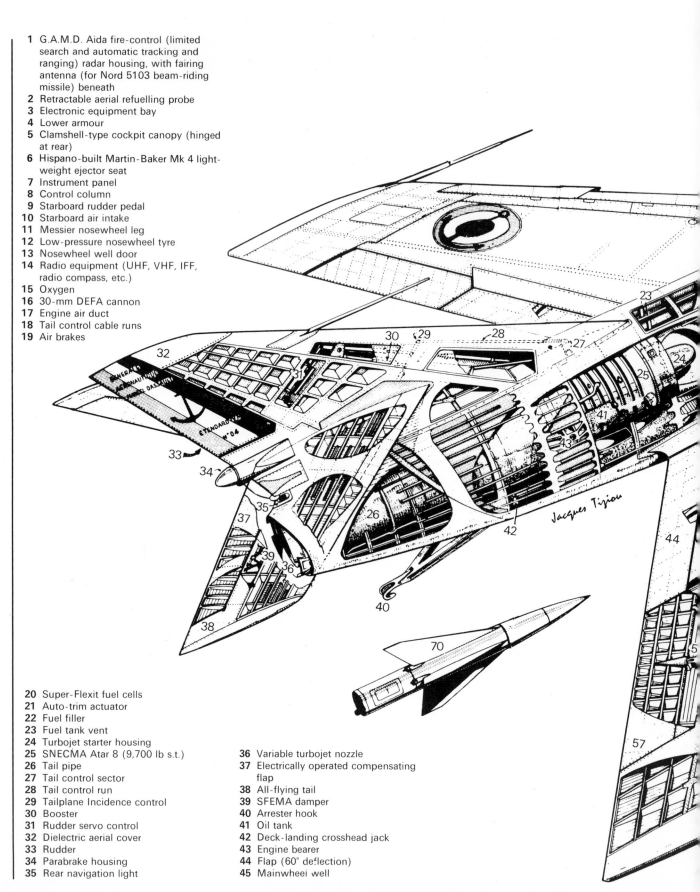

1 G.A.M.D. Aida fire-control (limited
   search and automatic tracking and
   ranging) radar housing, with fairing
   antenna (for Nord 5103 beam-riding
   missile) beneath
2 Retractable aerial refuelling probe
3 Electronic equipment bay
4 Lower armour
5 Clamshell-type cockpit canopy (hinged
   at rear)
6 Hispano-built Martin-Baker Mk 4 lightweight ejector seat
7 Instrument panel
8 Control column
9 Starboard rudder pedal
10 Starboard air intake
11 Messier nosewheel leg
12 Low-pressure nosewheel tyre
13 Nosewheel well door
14 Radio equipment (UHF, VHF, IFF,
   radio compass, etc.)
15 Oxygen
16 30-mm DEFA cannon
17 Engine air duct
18 Tail control cable runs
19 Air brakes

20 Super-Flexit fuel cells
21 Auto-trim actuator
22 Fuel filler
23 Fuel tank vent
24 Turbojet starter housing
25 SNECMA Atar 8 (9,700 lb s.t.)
26 Tail pipe
27 Tail control sector
28 Tail control run
29 Tailplane Incidence control
30 Booster
31 Rudder servo control
32 Dielectric aerial cover
33 Rudder
34 Parabrake housing
35 Rear navigation light

36 Variable turbojet nozzle
37 Electrically operated compensating
   flap
38 All-flying tail
39 SFEMA damper
40 Arrester hook
41 Oil tank
42 Deck-landing crosshead jack
43 Engine bearer
44 Flap (60° deflection)
45 Mainwheel well

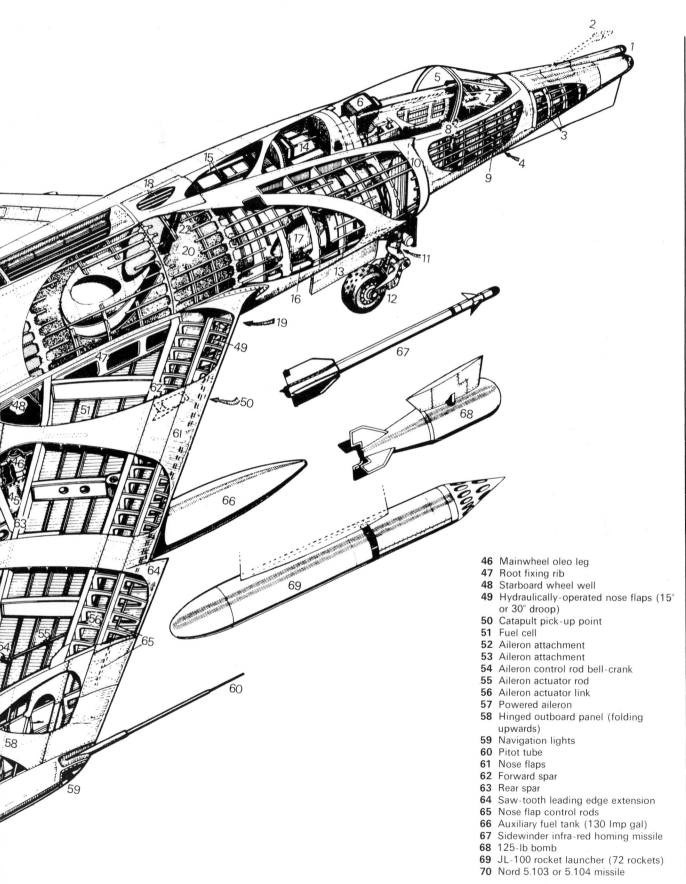

46 Mainwheel oleo leg
47 Root fixing rib
48 Starboard wheel well
49 Hydraulically-operated nose flaps (15°
    or 30° droop)
50 Catapult pick-up point
51 Fuel cell
52 Aileron attachment
53 Aileron attachment
54 Aileron control rod bell-crank
55 Aileron actuator rod
56 Aileron actuator link
57 Powered aileron
58 Hinged outboard panel (folding
    upwards)
59 Navigation lights
60 Pitot tube
61 Nose flaps
62 Forward spar
63 Rear spar
64 Saw-tooth leading edge extension
65 Nose flap control rods
66 Auxiliary fuel tank (130 Imp gal)
67 Sidewinder infra-red homing missile
68 125-lb bomb
69 JL-100 rocket launcher (72 rockets)
70 Nord 5.103 or 5.104 missile

Genesis

The Etendard (which means 'standard' or 'flag'), like the Super Etendard, is a product of the design team of Avions Marcel Dassault, the fiercely independent and pragmatic company built up by its founder to occupy a commanding place in the European aviation industry against nationalised competition. 'D'Assault', (the expression *char d'assaut* means 'tank' in French), was the Resistance code name of Marcel's brother, Paul Bloch. Following the liberation both brothers changed their original name of Bloch to Dassault. In fact Marcel Bloch built his first aircraft in 1918, a two-seat reconnaissance machine designed in partnership with Henry Potez. The first SE-4 flew just as the armistice ended the war and with it the manufacture of combat aircraft. For ten years Marcel Bloch concentrated on making furniture while his erstwhile partner Potez became Europe's largest aircraft manufacturer.

By 1930 Bloch was back in the aircraft business, designing and building civil and military aircraft until in 1936, with the prospect of war in Europe looming, the company was nationalised as the Societé Nationale des Constructions Aeronautiques du Sud 'Ouest.

In 1940 Bloch fighters were among the most modern aircraft facing the Luftwaffe but many were caught on the ground as France collapsed. However, the new Bloch 152 radial-engined fighters acquitted themselves well, shooting down 188 enemy aircraft for the loss of 86.

Bloch survived imprisonment by the Vichy French and the appalling deprivations of a Nazi concentration camp. He returned to find the French aero industry either stripped by the retreating invaders or smashed by Allied bombing. It had to be rebuilt from the ground up, just as the technical advances of the war meant building a whole new aero-engine and airframe technology in the heady new environment of jet propulsion and aerodynamics for supersonic flight and beyond.

German research provided a head start, of course, and the US, Soviet, British and French were already squabbling over the spoils. The French plucked the chief technical engineer of BMW, Paul Oestrich, from under the noses of the Americans and, together with 150 German engineers, work began on a new generation of jet engines at the old Dornier factory at Lindau-Rickenbach, in the French zone of occupation. The unit was called 'Atelier Aéronautique de Rickenbach' and the initials were combined to spell 'Atar'. The Atar engine which powers the Super Etendard built by SNECMA (Société Nationale d'Etude et de Construction de Moteurs d'Aviation, a nationalised company based on the old Gnome-Rhône concern) is a descendant of that original single-spool military turbojet first run in 1948.

France meanwhile had to rebuild her armed forces and their manufacturing base. Looming on the political horizon were the cold-war nuclear preoccupations of the 1950s and the bloody entanglements of colonial disengagement, first in Indo-China and then in Algeria, punctuated by the Suez fiasco of 1956.

The planners of France's reborn armed forces were determined to make them once again an instrument capable of world-wide power projection and, as important, to acquire nuclear weapons and the means to deliver them as expeditiously as possible. Aircraft carriers and naval aircraft fitted both these prescriptions.

In fact, in the immediate post-war period, the aircraft carrier was seen very much as a nuclear delivery platform. The US Navy got there in 1949 with the AJ Savage, a piston- and jet-engined bomber capable of carrying a cumbersome nuclear weapon weighing 10,000 lb (4,536 kg) on shallow missions into the Soviet Union. In the 1950s, however, just as the Soviets were perfecting their own nuclear bomb and beginning to embark on bomber and missile programmes for intercontinental delivery, the design weight of tactical nuclear bombs fell dramatically. By 1955 virtually any US Navy carrier fighter was capable of the nuclear mission. As a result the Soviet Navy was pushed on to the defensive, deploying a large fleet of submarines as 'carrier-killers'. Only now is the Soviet Navy working on conventional fixed-wing naval aircraft and a nuclear-powered carrier.

The French Navy had been taking aircraft to sea since May 1914 when the first launch was made from the deck of the converted torpedo depot ship *Forbin*. There were more experiments after the First World War, until in 1927 the unfinished battleship *Béarn* was completed (with British technical assistance) as an aircraft carrier proper with an air group of 40 machines. The small size of the naval air arm meant that several promising prototypes could not be put into production and thus the aircraft actually in service up to 1939 were largely obsolescent. This factor of small size and thus a small funding constituency for purpose-designed carrier aircraft was to re-emerge postwar and figure largely in the Etendard story.

In 1936 planning began for new carriers and two 18,000-ton vessels, the *Joffre* and *Painlevé*, were authorised in 1937. The fall of France truncated these plans although design work ticked over during the Occupation.

Left: The Super Etendard is one of the few supersonic aircraft in the world to use a non-afterburning engine, namely the SNECMA Atar 8K-50. This is in essence the unaugmented version of the Atar 9K-50, and weighs 2,546 lb (1,155 kg) with all accessories. It is 12 ft 11 in (3.936 m) long and has a diameter of 40.2 in (1.02 m). At a thrust rating of 11,023 lb (5,000 kg), the Atar 8K-50 has a specific fuel consumption of 0.97 lb/hour/lb static thrust (27.5 mg/Ns).

Below left: The SNECMA Atar 9C, itself a development of the Atar 9B and precursor of the Atar 9K-50 and thus of the Atar 8K-50. Compared with the Atar 9B the Atar 9C introduced a self-contained starter and a new compressor.

Below: SNECMA Atar 8K-50 (with core below) showing the unaugmented jetpipe and plain nozzle.

After 1944, studies were made for converting the incomplete battleship *Jean Bart* to an aircraft carrier while naval planners drew up an ambitious plan to equip the reborn French Navy with no less than six carriers. In 1947, however, the French Parliament approved construction of just one ship and even this was cancelled in 1950 due to lack of funds. But war in Indo-China, halfway round the world, meant the French Navy had to get back into the carrier business quickly. The ex-British light fleet carrier *Colossus* was lent to France in 1946, renamed *Arromanches*, and purchased outright in 1951. The light escort carrier HMS *Biter* was meanwhile acquired as the *Dixmude*. Two war-built light carriers of the *Independence*-class were supplied by the United States in 1953 and renamed *Bois Belleau* and *Lafayette* (returned in 1960 and 1963 respectively).

In the Indo-China war the French Aéronavale was equipped with Second World War-vintage US-types such as the Vought F4U Corsair and Douglas Dauntless and in fact the last F4U was retired from service as late as 1964.

Since 1945 the basic concepts of carrier and carrier-aircraft design had advanced significantly. The advent of jet aircraft with much higher operating weights and speeds and the realisation that naval aircraft had to compete and survive in combat with land based counterparts meant not just a revolution in aircraft but in the ships that operated them. Three British inventions, the angle-deck, the steam catapult and the mirror landing sight, allowed a quickening in the tempo of operations plus the capacity to launch much heavier aircraft and these became by the late 1950s standard equipment on all new carriers geared to jet operations. Second World War veterans were no longer enough.

Naval aircraft had always imposed very special design constraints which rule out the simple adaptation of land-based counterparts. Naval aircraft have to be especially tough and rugged to withstand the shocks of launch and arrested landing ('controlled crashes' in US Navy terminology). High performance jets have to be built to withstand the stresses of high manoeuvring anyway, so this factor is not as important as formerly, although still significant. The airframe must be light and strong yet resistant to the corrosive atmosphere on a carrier, where salt water spray eats into aluminium and magnesium alloys. Dimensions are critical to fit carrier deck lifts and hangar height and the lifts and flight deck themselves impose weight limits.

A catapult shot punches the aircraft from zero to 140 knots in about 1.5 seconds and most of this load is on the nose wheel where it engages the catapult. An arrested landing reverses the

Real precursor of the naval Etendard series was the Etendard IV light tactical fighter prototype, which was larger, heavier and more powerful than the Etendard II.

Features well displayed on this Etendard IVM are the broad fuselage, wide-track landing gear and Vee-type retractable arrester hook. Note also the drop-tanks.

process, decelerating the aircraft from 130 knots to zero in 1.5 seconds. The punishment does not stop there. The sink rate of an Etendard landing is about 28 feet per second. As it hits the flight deck, the wing tips flex up, then momentum brings them down, travelling through an arc of two to three feet.

Carrier landing requires good low speed performance but combat efficiency requires the best performance at high speed and high altitude; the designer of naval aircraft has to find the right compromise. Naval aircraft need long range and loiter time — to fit in with the carrier operating cycle, to mount combat air

patrols for effective fleet air defence, or in the case of surface strike aircraft such as the Super Etendard, to make long over-water search and strike missions.

The advent of jet engines created new design compli-cations. Piston engines driving variable pitch propellers have a wide band of efficiency at various power settings. Jet engines, in contrast, have only two modes of operation — normal thrust which provides power for subsonic flight and afterburner which is generally used only for short periods to blast the aircraft through Mach speed and beyond. Once the afterburner is lit, how-ever, fuel is gulped down and for a small aircraft the effect on range is critical. Neither the Etendard nor the Super Etendard has an afterburning engine, hence speed is just transonic. In fact

the Super Etendard of 1979 is barely faster than the Etendard IVM of 1962, but it has far greater range and combat capability.

The French Navy in the late 'forties was anxious to cast off its rag-bag of secondhand carriers and flying veterans and begin building modern ships and aircraft as rapidly as possible. Meanwhile, as shown, virtually all the design rules had changed and, with low production runs, purpose-built carrier aircraft along US or British lines were going to be prohibitively expensive. Nevertheless the ambitious re-armament programme of 1946 called for the construction of 70 naval fighters (the unusual twin boom pusher SO 8000 Narval) and 105 twin-engined bombers (Nord NC 1050), both compara-tively large and long-ranged.

Above: Least successful of the Etendard
prototypes was the Etendard II, powered
by a pair of unreliable Gabizo turbojets.
Below: The protuberant cockpit of the
Etendard II provided good fields of vision,
while the slim nose was indicative of the
lack of radar.

However ambitious, this was still only the interim as very soon the French Navy issued orders for its first jets. These were the Arsenal VG 90, Nord 2200 and NC 1080 fighter bombers and the first French twin-jet, the Nord 1071. Take-off characteristics of the prototypes were poor and the cash demands of the Indo-China war caused the cancellation of all naval jet fighter projects by 1953.

The only survivor of this period was the Br 960 Vultur turboprop-powered strike bomber, similar in concept to the British Westland Wyvern. In fact in 1952 the French Navy gave priority to the anti-submarine mission and the Vultur emerged later, heavily modified, as the Alizé ASW aircraft which still serves on French and Indian carriers.

Thus the Aéronavale's first operational jet was the British

Much had been expected of the reheated version of the Gabizo (as illustrated here), but the type was plagued with problems and eventually abandoned, generally in favour of larger engines for higher performance.

Sea Venom, built under license as the Sud Aquilon. By the mid-1950s it seemed there was no longer any prospect of specialised naval aircraft – the navy would have to become the suppliant customer joining the end of the production runs for the Armée de l'Air. The new jets entering service with the air force, the Dassault Ouragan and Mystère IV, were meanwhile studied and rejected as unsuitable for carrier operations.

Where to turn next? In 1954 a new French-built carrier was approved by Parliament and a second in 1955. These were completed as the *Clémenceau* and *Foch* in 1959 and 1963 respectively, both displacing 32,800 tons and with a capacity for 30 aircraft, and fitted with British Mitchell-Brown steam catapults capable of handling aircraft up to 11 tons all-up weight. By comparison, contemporary US aircraft carriers of the *Constellation* class were built with more than double the displacement and capacity for 90 aircraft. The Royal Navy's *Ark Royal* completed in 1955 had a

displacement of 53,786 tons and capacity for 36 aircraft. The new French carriers were comparatively small, which made the adoption of land aircraft programmes even more problematic.

Then in December 1953 NATO announced a contest for a lightweight strike fighter to have short field take-off capability. The French entries were the Breguet Br 1001 Taon and the Générale Aeronautique Marcel Dassault Mystère XXVI, later renamed Etendard. In fact three different fighter prototypes, all dubbed Etendard, were built and flown by Dassault in 1955–7. They shared a broadly similar airframe with swept wings, and powerplant buried in the fuselage fed by cheek intakes. The Etendard VI was powered by a Bristol Siddeley Orpheus engine of 4,850-lb (2,200-kg) thrust and was the unsuccessful NATO contest entry. The Etendard II was powered by twin 2,420-lb (1,097-kg) thrust Turboméca Gabizo turbojets and was designed to meet an Armée de l'Air requirement for a lightweight strike fighter.

Above: The Etendard VI was based on the Etendard II, but the two Gabizos were supplanted by a single Bristol Siddeley Orpheus for generally improved performance.
Below: The meaning of Etendard is 'war flag', leading to the nice nose insignia of the Etendard VI.

Development

The Etendard II first flew on 23 July 1955 at Melun Villaroche but was abandoned after a brief test period. The aircraft was underpowered and the air force meanwhile had lost interest in the light fighter and were much more interested in Dassault's potent Mirage III. When official NATO and air force funding dried up, Dassault did not abandon the Etendard but privately funded the development of the aircraft with a much more powerful engine. A single SNECMA Atar 101E3 engine of 9,700 lb (4,400 kg) thrust was installed and the Etendard IV was born. The handsome aircraft first flew at Bordeaux-Merignac on 24 July 1956 and the bigger engine at last brought out all the potential of the airframe. The Aéronavale sat up and took

The Etendard IV prepares for a sortie. Note the stored Dassault-Breguet Mystère IVA fighters in the background, with cockpits and inlets protected against the weather.

notice of the private venture prototype — it was small and it was a single-seater with all the problems of navigation and weapon management set on the pilot. It was single-engined with the risks of over-water reliability — but it was affordable and it was French.

The subsonic Etendard was not considered at first as a replacement for the ageing Sud Aquilon. That was to be a new aircraft capable of Mach 1.8 and of carrying a nuclear weapon which the French were very near to developing. In fact before the French Navy began developing ballistic missile submarines, carrier aircraft were planned as an important component of the nuclear deterrent and a very large ship was planned in 1958–61, capable of operating a naval version of the large Mirage IV strategic nuclear bomber.

The big carrier was cancelled in 1961 and the proposed supersonic nuclear-strike aircraft, either the Breguet Br 1120 Sirocco or a navalised Mirage III, were cancelled soon afterwards, leaving the Etendard to soldier on

alone until the Aéronavale bought the US Crusader F-8 supersonic fighter in 1963.

Soon after the first flight of the Atar-powered Etendard IV-01 prototype on 24 July 1956, Dassault was given the go-ahead to build a semi-navalised prototype and six fully-navalised pre-production aircraft of a type named Etendard IVM (for Marine). Still not satisfied, Dassault's team installed a Rolls-Royce Avon 51 engine producing 11,250 lb (5,100 kg) thrust into the third aircraft, to produce the Etendard IVB. The extra power was used to blow high pressure air across the wing leading edges and flaps to produce an artificial airflow across the wings, allowing the IVB to land some 30 to 40 knots slower than Etendards without blown-wings and to use the 103-ft (31.4-m) catapult of the smaller carriers. In fact these were on the way to being scrapped or converted to ASW helicopter carriers and so the IVB proved unnecessary, although it was a technical *tour de force* for the time in such a small aircraft.

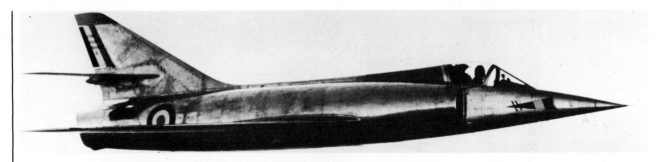

Above: The Etendard IV at speed for the benefit of the camera crew.
Left: One of the features of the Etendard IVM series is the provision for inflight-refuelling equipment above the nose, and the perforated ventral airbrakes under the wing.
Below: The fairing at the junction of the vertical and horizontal tail surfaces of the Etendard IVM houses the braking parachute, the fairing being closed by a small cap until the parachute is used.

Seen on a training mission in France, the Argentinian navy's first Super Etendards fly in close formation. Despite their small numbers, these aircraft played an important part in the Falklands campaign of 1982, their Exocet anti-ship missiles offering one of the greatest threats to the Royal Navy's South Atlantic Task Force.

Left: A SNECMA Atar 9K-50, the reheated version of the engine used in the Super Etendard strike fighter.
Above right: Super Etendard no. 37 is seen as part of the static display at an air display at Greenham Common in the UK.
Right: The two most important guided weapons used by the Super Etendard are the Matra 550 Magic dogfighting air-to-air missile and the Aérospatiale AM.39 Exocet anti-ship missile. They are seen here at the Paris Air Show, 1983.
Below: The Super Etendard is well suited to carrier operations by virtue of its sturdy wide-track landing gear and advanced high-lift devices.

All ready for the launch of Super Etendard no. 7, with steam rising from the catapult system and the engine fully run up.
Inset left: The clean lines of the Super Etendard are well shown in this view of the undersurfaces.

Left: A Super Etendard rises up from the hangar deck on one of a French carrier's two lifts.
Below left: Deck handling and parking are two important aspects of aircraft-carrier management, for only thus can maximum numbers of aircraft such as these Super Etendards be deployed aboard the limited space available.
Right: A mood shot aboard a French carrier with Super Etendard strike fighters.
Below: The moment of commitment as a Super Etendard is about to be catapulted along the angle flight deck. Note the high angle of attack provided by the long nose-wheel leg, and maximum 'up' elevator.

Above: Escorted by four companions, a pair of Super Etendards shows off the Douglas-designed 'buddy' inflight-refuelling technique to extend the combat radius of warplanes with extra fuel from a similar type.

Left: Super Etendards are seen in the course of an inflight-refuelling exercise.

Facing page:

Top: The Etendard IV prototype (no. 01) first flew on 24 July 1956, being followed by the Etendard IVM-01 on 21 May 1958.

Centre: Characteristics of all the more modern of Dassault's aircraft have been a cleanness of line, and the re-use of successful features. This is the Etendard IV at moderately high speed.

Bottom: Seen aboard the carrier *Clémenceau* is some of her powerful air group, including five Vought F-8E(FN) fighters, six Breguet Alizé anti-submarine aircraft and 15 Etendard IVM strike fighters.

The naval prototype, Etendard IVM-01, flew for the first time on 21 May 1958 from Melun-Villaroche, the five pre-production aircraft following during 1959–60. The principal modification from Etendard IV to IVM included the provision of an arrester hook, catapult spools, a long-stroke main undercarriage with high-pressure tyres, folding wingtips, Ai'da 7 lightweight radar, retractable flight refuelling probe, two perforated ventral air-brakes and a high lift system using leading edge and trailing edge wing flaps.

Structurally the Etendard IVM was conventional — a metal semi-monocoque fuselage which was waisted to conform to area rule aerodynamics. The two spar wings were swept back from quarter-chord at 45 degrees and equipped with hydraulically-powered ailerons and powered spoilers ahead of double slotted flaps (maximum deflection 60°) and powered leading edge flaps (maximum deflection 30°). Spoilers were often used to improve lateral control and increase roll-rate.

The wing aspect ratio was 3, while thickness-chord ratio varied from 6 to 5 from root to tip with a slight anhedral of 3° 30'. The tail section housed a brake parachute at the junction of the fin and the one-piece, all-flying tailplane.

After four months of manufacturer's trials which included some fifty test flights, the prototype was passed to the Centre d'Essais en Vol at Istres where official testing began in October 1958. Then aircraft IVM-01 came to RAE, Bedford, England, for catapult and arrested landing trials.

The first pre-production aircraft, the Etendard IVM-02 completed initial carrier qualifications aboard the brand new *Clémenceau* between 19 and 24 September 1960. This aircraft, like the four later pre-production machines, was powered by the 9,700-lb

Among the Etendard IVM's weapons fit are two 30-mm cannon (under the fuselage) and, working outwards, 500- and 1,000-lb (227- and 454-kg) bombs, AS.20 missiles, LR150 rocket-launcher pods, and drop-tanks.

(4,400-kg) thrust Atar O8 which was to be adopted as the production standard.

The first production Etendard IVM flew in July 1961 and soon afterwards deliveries were made to Flotille 15F, which served as the operational training unit. Flotille 11F, embarked aboard *Foch*, was the next unit to equip, and Flotilles 14F and 17F finally replaced their veteran F4U-7 Corsairs during 1964.

The Etendard IVM was a strike aircraft with a secondary air-to-air function. Armament was two 30-mm DEFA cannon, each with 150 rounds, and the aircraft had four underwing pylons to carry up to 3,000 lb (1,360 kg) of bombs, rocket pods or air-to-air missiles such as the AIM-9 Sidewinder. The Nord AS.20 air-to-surface missile was another armament option and the characteristic blade fairing beneath the Etendard IVM's nose was the

antenna for this weapon's radio command guidance. Alternatively, the aircraft could carry more fuel in two 130-Imp gal (600-litre) drop tanks, supplementing the 720 Imp gal (3,300 litres) carried internally and there was a retractable in-flight refuelling probe carried just ahead of the cockpit.

The mission avionics of the IVM were relatively advanced with an Ai'da 7 intercept and ground ranging radar, Tacan, which is a navigational aid allowing the pilot to find his range and bearing from a coded beacon. A SAAB Type BT9F analogue computer enabled the aircraft to make toss-bomb stand-off attacks with conventional and, later, nuclear weapons.

There was another variation on the Etendard IV theme, the reconnaissance and tanker variant known as the Etendard IVP. The final pre-production aircraft, designated Etendard IVP-07 and first flown on 19 November 1960, was modified to carry three OMERA cameras in the nose and a twin vertical camera installation in the bay

normally occupied by the IVM's cannon. The Etendard IVP was also equipped with a fixed flight refuelling probe in place of the normal Ai'da 7 nose radar. To provide in-flight refuelling, the IVP carried a Douglas-designed hose/reel pod on a centreline pylon, plus two drop tanks. Some 21 Etendard IVPs were produced and served on both carriers, tanking IVMs and F-8 Crusaders as well as providing pre- and post-strike reconnaissance. The 'buddy pack' refuelling capacity was extended to the Super Etendard and was to prove crucial during the Falklands operations.

The initial export potential of the Etendard IVM looked good, especially as other naval air arms were, by the early 1960s, equipping with naval jets but with small Second World War-vintage carriers from which small aircraft could operate. However, although Australia (with the *Melbourne* and *Sydney*) nearly bought the aircraft, they pulled out in 1963, only to order the US A-4 Skyhawk later. The Brazilian carrier *Minas Gerais* was an ASW platform only. The Indians could

Above: Deck crew attach the catapult strop to Etendard IVM no. 36, seen with the seahorse insignia of 11 Flotille on the tail. Note the scale of marks by the all-moving tailplane to indicate angle.

Above left: Etendard IVM no. 22 lifts off the flight deck of the carrier *Clémenceau* for a training mission with an underwing load of just two drop-tanks.

Left: Deck crew work on a pair of Etendard IVP photographic reconnaissance aircraft on the strength of 16 Flotille. Well displayed are the port and oblique windows on each side of the noses of both aircraft. Armament comprises underwing rocket-launchers.

Below: The carrier *Clémenceau* comes into port with her sides manned, helicopters amidships by the island, Alizés at the stern and Etendard IVMs at the bow.

not afford a replacement for the Supermarine Seahawks embarked on *Vikrant* although they had bought Alizé ASW aircraft. Argentina had only just acquired an aircraft carrier with the purchase in 1958 of an ex-British light fleet carrier HMS *Warrior*, renamed *Indepencia*. The Royal Netherlands Navy was pulling out of operating carriers and were to sell the *Karel Doorman* to Argentina as the *Veinticinco de Mayo* in 1968. The Argentinian Aviacion Naval's first equipment was ancient F4U-5 and -5N Corsair fighter bombers and then in 1962 twenty Grumman F9F-2 Panthers were acquired from US surplus. High technology naval aircraft were still a long way from Argentina's reach.

Thus the Aéronavale was eventually the only customer for

the Etendard IVM and IVP, 69 and 21 of which were delivered respectively. The production line closed in 1962.

The Etendard IVM was very much a strike aircraft, similar to a smaller version of the Royal Navy's Buccaneer and not suited to the air-to-air role. As described, French attempts to develop an indigenous fleet air defence aircraft in the 1950s had been unsuccessful and the carriers were too small to operate a large multi-purpose aircraft, such as the Phantom eventually bought by the Royal Navy.

A project in 1960 was for a 'Talp' aircraft (*tactique à longue portée* or tactical aircraft of long range) which was to be a combination of a relatively slow weapon platform armed with air-to-air missiles of advanced capability. A modified Etendard with four-hour endurance and a large radar was considered, but the project was abandoned. In 1963 the French Navy decided to buy the US Crusader as a carrier-based fleet fighter and a special version, the F-8E (FN) was built, equipped with a new APQ-104 radar compatible with the French MATRA R-530 air-to-air missile. The French carriers' small size again showed itself as a design constraint and the F-8 was reworked to create a reduction in landing speed by at least 15 knots. To this end the F-8E (FN) was given increased wing camber, flap blowing, doubled aileron and flap deflection, a 20% reduction in wing incidence travel and increased horizontal tail surfaces.

There was a last attempt in 1963–4 at an indigenous French naval fighter which would combine long range and high performance and yet be operable from the small carriers. The twin Spey-powered Breguet Br 120 was designed to attain Mach 2.4 at altitude with variable geometry for low landing speeds. The Mirage G, built to the same

specification, flew in 1967, attained Mach 2.5 and yet was able to land at a leisurely 110 knots. However, neither proceeded beyond a prototype as the demands of building up France's strategic nuclear forces

An Etendard IVM makes a pass over the carrier *Clémenceau*. The starboard spoiler, just ahead of the special double-slotted flaps, is raised slightly.

Armament of the Etendard IV was a pair of 30-mm DEFA cannon.

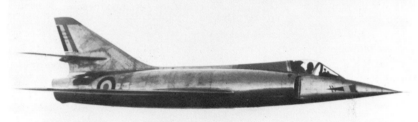

had severely curtailed available cash for these very ambitious but small-run variable geometry projects.

Thus there was no planned replacement for the now-ageing Etendard IVM and by the late 1960s the French Navy had to think hard about what it could afford next. The old problem of small numbers pushed up unit costs and yet the size of the carriers imposed restrictions on simply navalising land-based types, or going for bigger and heavier dual purpose interceptor/

ground attack aircraft. In 1968 a naval version of the Anglo-French Jaguar strike trainer was ordered and the aircraft, designated Jaguar M, first flew on 14 November 1969. It was stressed for carrier operations and had a beefed-up undercarriage but, partly for political reasons, the Jaguar M programme was abandoned in 1970.

It was deemed that with more capable weapon systems a supersonic platform was unnecessary. The Vought A-7 Corsair II was studied, as was

Top: Three Etendard IVPs trail a trio of Etendard IVMs (nos 16, 42 and 62).
Centre: Etendard IV with airbrake deployed.
Above: An Etendard IVM formates on Concorde.

the Etendard's old adversary the A-4 Skyhawk, and in fact a special French version received the designation A-4T. It was argued that 100 A-4s would be less expensive than 70 French-built equivalents. This kind of argument was of course anathema to those concerned – not just France's defence chiefs

The number 102 indicates that this machine is an Etendard IVP, written off on 26 August 1971 while on the strength of 16 Flotille.

but the domestic industries which supported them — and Dassault in particular.

The formidable old pragmatist had an alternative solution. Take the proven Etendard airframe and re-equip it with a new engine and a new fit of multi-function avionics. Combine it with an air-launched version of Aérospatiale's Exocet anti-ship missile or Matra Magic air-to-air missiles and you had a combination of weapon system and weapon platform entirely capable of carrying forward the French Navy's strike and fleet air defence mission. Furthermore the aircraft could carry AN52 thermonuclear weapons in the nuclear strike role. Thus it was the Super Etendard was born.

As the specification for the Super Etendard was being written in the early 70s, the whole future of the conventional take-off and landing (CTOL) aircraft carrier was in the melting pot. The US Navy remained committed to nuclear-powered super-carriers, and the Soviet Navy equally committed to missile-equipped attack submarines to destroy them.

The British Government, however, had cancelled the Royal Navy's forward carrier programme in 1966 although the so-called 'through-deck cruiser' was to emerge later as the VTOL-carrying *Invincible* class, equipped with Sea Harriers.

France, similarly faced with prohibitive costs, a dwindling

world role and an ever-increasing emphasis on submarine warfare decided, like the Royal Navy, to concentrate on submarines, with missile ships and helicopter-carriers in the surface role. In 1974 it looked as if the two CTOL carriers would be run on to the natural end of their hull lives and be replaced by a new kind of ship — a nuclear-powered helicopter/VTOL carrier called PA 75. In fact, as discussed later, this policy has been overturned and France is planning to build two nuclear-powered carriers to enter service in 1990 — but here again was an imperative to go for the quick-fix Super Etendard solution rather than an ambitious home-grown supersonic variable geometry project.

Etendard IVM into Super Etendard

Dassault's original proposal was simply to install new avionics, radar and weapon systems into the original Etendard IVM, making the Super Etendard 90% common with its progenitor. In fact the changes grew until the aircraft was 90% new.

The engine was changed. The Atar 8 was replaced by the 11,025-lb (4,900-kg) thrust Atar 8K-50, essentially the 9K-50 powerplant of the Mirage F.1 but without the afterburner. The new engine has a lower specific fuel consumption and thus affords greater range, and the maintenance effort is claimed to be half its predecessor's. The thrust increase of 10% is also critical in allowing a significant increase in all-up weight for catapulting, again making possible an increase in fuel load and thus in range.

The fuselage was redesigned to accommodate the new engine, the air intakes and ducting were enlarged and the tail was re-profiled around the fixed non-afterburning engine exhaust nozzle, with a brake parachute in a housing at the tail surfaces' intersection. The front end was remodelled around the new radar.

The airframe was redesigned and strengthened in places for operation at the higher speeds and weights which the increased power afforded. The wing was substantially redesigned with comprehensive high-lift devices, leading edge wing blowing, leading edge droops for more lift, spoilers ahead of the flaps for increased roll control and new double-slotted blown flaps similar to those developed originally for the Jaguar M.

These aerodynamic modifications allow the Super Etendard to take off at higher weights than the Etendard IVM (26,455 lb/ 11,900 kg compared to 22,650 lb/ 10,200 kg). The blown wing kept the approach speed at 135 knots (250 km/h) for an aircraft with fuel and stores expended weighing 17,200 lb (7,800 kg), comparing well with the lighter Etendard IVM.

Large air brakes deploying from the belly can produce a deceleration of 0.4 g while the undercarriage, designed and built by Messier-Hispano, is particularly robust with long stroke shock absorbers and medium pressure tyres.

The essence of a modern strike aircraft's combat power is its fit of electronics — for navigation, target acquisition and weapon aiming. From 1972 the French electronics company Thomson-CSF had been working on a lightweight multifunction radar called Vigie, which showed considerable promise in prototype form. In 1973 Thomson-CSF joined with Electronique Marcel Dassault to develop the system for the Super Etendard under the name 'Agave'. The Agave, despite its small size and weight, is a true multifunction radar making extensive use of solid state micro-circuitry and is designed for easy maintenance.

Basic functions of the Agave are air-to-surface search and air-to-air search; target designation for the homing head of a long range active homing missile; or, linked to the cockpit head-up display (HUD), automatic air-to-surface or air-to-air tracking, air-to-air and air-to-ground rangefinding, and map display. The Agave can be used in the ground mapping mode, searching through 70 degrees either side of the nose and 60 degrees in pitch to provide update fixes for the aircraft's inertial navigational system. Other optional air-to-surface modes include contour mapping and bad weather terrain following, providing (via the onboard computer) steering and pitch references to the head-up display, itself new on the Super Etendard.

In the air-to-air mode, the detection range for a fighter aircraft is within 11–17 miles (18–28 km). In the air-to-surface mode the range is about 30 miles (48 km) for a patrol boat and more than 60 miles (96 km) for a destroyer the size of HMS *Sheffield*, for example. An optional wide antenna increases

The prototype Super Etendard, seen with gear retracting, was converted from Etendard IVM no. 68.

Left: One of the keys to the superior operational capability of the Super Etendard series is the Thomson-CSF/EMD Agave lightweight multi-role radar, whose basic functions are air-to-air search, air-to-surface search, target designation, automatic air-to-air tracking, automatic air-to-surface tracking and map display.
Right: The antenna of the Agave radar is of the inverse Cassegrain type, stabilized in roll and pitch, and among the Agave's optional modes are contour mapping and blind penetration. The weight of the whole system is 143 lb (65 kg), of which 106 lb (48 kg) is in the nosecone and the rest in the cockpit and fuselage.
Below: An Etendard IVM lands on board the carrier *Clémenceau.*

The first production Super Etendard passes across the stern of the carrier *Clémenceau*.

these ranges. In the search mode the Agave scans 70 degrees either side of the line of flight and 60 degrees in elevation. Within this arc the actual angle of search is either 6 degrees or twelve degrees depending on whether a one- or two-bar scan pattern is used. In practice a one-bar pattern is automatically selected for low level work and at altitude a two-bar pattern cuts in to improve close-in coverage. The pilot has the option of moving this scan pattern up or down through the full 60 degrees.

The Agave system is highly automated. It has an instantaneous automatic gain control which sorts out target reflections from wave or ground clutter and displays them sharply. If the ground mapping mode is used, the best possible tracking elevation for the optimum coverage of the ground ahead of the aircraft is automatically set up.

Once in the air, the pilot selects the mode and range to be scanned — air-to-surface or air-to-air — and the range from five to 80 nautical miles.

For a single seat aircraft, operating over water, the navigation equipment must be to a high standard. The rather basic navigational fit of the Etendard IVM centred on the Tacan receiver, which depended on ground beacons from which it worked out its range and bearing. Two decades later the technology has moved on and now allows comparatively small aircraft to carry a sophisticated and highly accurate inertial navigation system (INS), a system of accelerometers and gyroscopes, controlled by computer. By 'knowing' where it started from it can determine its present position by computing how far, how fast and in which directions it has travelled. Wind and instrument error can lead the INS astray over a long distance (1.2 nm per hour in the Super Etendard) but it can be fed with updated information either by the pilot overflying a known fixed point or being fed accurate radar ranging fixes from Agave.

The controlling brain of all this is the INS-attack computer called 'Etna' built by SAGEM under

Airbrakes deployed, flaps lowered and arrester hook ready to latch onto the wires, an Etendard IVM ends a sortie.

Super Etendards on the production line against a backdrop of Dassault-Breguet Mystère/Falcon executive jets.

licence from Singer-Kearfott. The Etna is made up of four units — the inertial navigation unit comprising two gyros and three accelerometers on a four axis platform; the weapon delivery computer; the control display unit; and an interface unit.

On the ground it takes about eight minutes to spin the gyros and align the Etna with information on its starting point; it takes slightly longer when at sea. When the aircraft is embarked aboard the carrier, the Etna is plugged into the ship's own INS which imparts a fix. This information is constantly updated by the Etna until the aircraft is launched, when the system carries on giving the pilot a continuous report of his position. The Etna also imparts information to the INS guidance system on the AM.39 air-launched Exocet missile when it is activated.

The Super Etendard's cockpit is completely new. It is extensively armoured and can afford protection against small calibre fire. The pilot has a head-up display which projects navigational data, aircraft management data and indication of horizon, speed, height and course onto a clear screen in the pilot's line of sight. The Agave feeds into the Thomson-CSF VE120 HUD and puts up weapon-aiming and target information on demand.

The pilot sits on a Martin Baker-type CM 4 ejection seat, licence built by Messier-Hispano. The Agave is controlled by a single stick to the pilot's left hand. Next to it is a small hand-controller to put navigation updates into the Etna system. On the right of the main panel is the Etna readout and data-entry keyboard for initial programming. To the right of the panel is the radar screen and above it is the head-up display. Other cockpit avionics include a Crouzet type 97 navigation display, armament control panel and selector box, a Crouzet type 66 air data computer, a TRT radio altimeter, flight, hydraulic and engine instruments by Jaeger and Tacan and IFF (Interrogation Friend or Foe) by LMT.

The Super Etendard has a wide range of armament options. It can carry the AN-52 tactical nuclear bomb with a yield of 15 kts. In fulfilling the air-to-air role, the Super Etendard retains the two 30-mm DEFA cannon with 125 rounds per gun and carries Matra R 550 Magic or Sidewinder heat-seeking air-to-air missiles on the outboard underwing pylons.

Of the four underwing pylons, the outer are cleared up to 1,000 lb (450 kg) and the inner two are cleared to 2,400 lb (1,300 kg) and plumbed for 240 Imp gal (1,100 litres) drop tanks. There is a double attachment point on the centreline, each

point having a 600 lb (250 kg) lift for bombs with alternatively a drop tank, a 'buddy' refuelling pack or a reconnaissance pod. The Super Etendard can carry an AM.39 Exocet under the starboard inner pylon, balanced by a 1,100 litres drop tank on the port inner pylon.

From the beginning of the

Super Etendard design programme it was intended to keep costs to a minimum and exploit the proven features of the Etendard IVM to the full. Super Etendard no. 01 was in fact the airframe of Etendard IVM no. 68 but fitted with the new Atar 8K-50. The first flight was on 28 October 1974 from the Dassault-

Among the weapons later qualified for the Etendard IVM series were the AIM-9 Sidewinder air-to-air missile and the AS.30 anti-ship missile.

Etendard IVM into Super Etendard

The eighth production example of the
Super Etendard is towed out of the
assembly building at Dassault-Breguet's
Bordeaux factory.

Breguet facility at Istres, with Jacques Jesberger at the controls. The flight was judged a complete success and a height of 44,000 feet was reached with a speed (in clean configuration) of Mach 1.18.

Super Etendard no. 02 was rebuilt from Etendard IVM no. 18. It also had the Atar 8K-50 but this time with certain aerodynamic changes to the fuselage including the intakes, the tail and the nose, which now contained the Agave nav-attack system which had been previously tested on a two-seat Jaguar. In fact no. 02 was preceded into the air on 9 March 1975 at Cazaux

by Super Etendard no. 03, fitted with the new wing with drooping leading edge and double slotted flaps. No. 03 was converted from Etendard IVM no. 13 and was still equipped with an original Atar 8C engine, but this machine was the test bed for the blown wing ('hypersustentation' in French).

In July 1975 Super Etendard no. 01 was fitted with no. 03's wing and no. 02's Agave nav-attack system, at last becoming the first true Super Etendard approaching production standard. By using Etendard IVM airframes, the Dassault team had produced virtually a completely new air-

craft within a remarkably short time — and within budget.

In November 1977 the first production aircraft began tests and on 28 June the first operational production Super Etendard was handed over to the French Navy.

The first two operational Super Etendards began evaluation flights in July 1978 before going to Flotille 11F, based at Landivisiau in Brittany, for working up. The first deck landing was aboard the carrier *Foch* on 4 December 1978, and by February 1979 11F had its full complement of 12 aircraft.

Flotille 14F, also based at
Landivisiau, converted from F-8
Crusaders in September 1979
and 17F, based at Hyères on the
Mediterranean coast, converted
from Etendard IVMs in July 1980.
It is planned to keep a squadron
each of Etendard IVM and IVPs
in service for some time, as
'buddy' tankers and reconnaissance aircraft respectively.
   Deliveries to the French Navy
continued through to late 1982,
making 71 aircraft in all. The
production line's last output was
an order for 14 from the
Argentinian Aviacion Naval — the
naval air force. The first was
delivered in 1980. The most
dramatic chapter in the story of
the Super Etendard was about to
begin.

Moments before the launch of an
Etendard IVM from the carrier *Foch*.

Above: Still trailing the arrester wire, an Etendard IVM comes to rest aboard an aircraft-carrier.

Left: Smoke puffing out from its main-wheels, the first prototype Super Etendard picks up the arrester wire during shipboard trials on a French carrier. Note the oddly shaped drop-tank on the centreline hardpoint.

Below: Compared with the photograph to the left, this captures the 17th production Super Etendard just a moment later as its nose wheel hits the deck. Note the drooped leading edges and the raised spoilers on the upper surfaces of the wing.

Right: All ready on the Super Etendard production line for the installation of the Atar 8K-50 into aircraft no. 9. Other points of interest are the lowered arrester hook, the open inspection panels and, on aircraft no. 10 in the background, the extended inflight-refuelling probe.

Top: Super Etendards on board the carrier *Clémenceau*, with (background and overhead) Vought F-8E(FN) Crusader fighters.
Above: An Etendard IVP of 16 Flotille at high speed just after picking up the arrester wire.
Left: Early production Super Etendard strike fighters prepare for a sortie. The aircraft in the foreground carries rocket-launcher pods, and the small amount of fold on the wingtips emphasises the overall compactness of the type.

Action in the South Atlantic

The Argentine Navy (*Armada Argentina*) is the sole export customer (to date) for the Super Etendard. All of the first batch of eight aircraft were delivered by 1 May 1982. At the time of writing, a total of 14 aircraft have been accepted by the navy's air arm (*Aviacion Naval Argentina*: ANA), the initial eight aircraft equipping the 2ª Escuadrilla de Caza y Ataque, an element within the 3ª Escuadra Aeronaval based at BAN Comandante Espora, Puerto Belgrano. The gathering pace of the Falklands conflict saw the 2ª Escuadrilla de Ataque redeploy to Rio Gallegos, with Rio Grande and Comodoro Rivadavia available as alternatives. Each of these bases was specially prepared to turn-round a Super Etendard at short notice, with particular emphasis on rapid and accurate alignment of the Etna INS and target-related computer programming. A second Super Etendard unit is now operational. Ultimately, one squadron is expected to embark aboard the aircraft carrier *Veinticinco de Mayo*, replacing Douglas A-4Q Skyhawks.

In virtually all respects the ANA's Super Etendards are identical to their French counterparts; notable exceptions include the deletion of all nuclear-arming and delivery capability, whether in the form of the ASMP stand-off missile, or the AN-52 free-fall bomb. MATRA R.550 Magic heat-seeking air-to-air missiles are included, although as yet the Argentines have not ordered this weapon. The only such missile in the Argentine arsenal is the outmoded AIM-9B Sidewinder of 1950s vintage. The standard armament of ANA Super Etendards is one AM.39 Exocet under the inner-starboard wing-pylon, balanced by an expend-able fuel tank beneath the opposite wing, and two DEFA 30-mm cannon.

Central to the ANA's plans for operating the Super Etendard is the 20,000 ton carrier *Veinticinco de Mayo* ('25th of May' – Argentine Independence Day). Launched on 30 December 1943 as HMS *Venerable*, she was bought by the Royal Netherlands Navy on 1 April 1948 and formally commissioned as the *Karel Doorman* eight weeks later. Argentina purchased the carrier on 15 October 1968 and the ship underwent a complete refit, including re-engining. A refit in 1955–8 had already given her an angled flight deck, a steam catapult and a new anti-aircraft gun battery and during her voyage from the Netherlands the *Veinticinco de Mayo* visited Portsmouth for catapult trials. Hawker Siddeley seized upon this opportunity to demonstrate a Harrier to the assembled chiefs of the Argentine Navy. Despite the fact that the Harrier GR.1 had only recently entered service with the RAF, and no naval version existed, the world's first operational V/STOL fighter flew out to the carrier in mid-Channel and impressed everyone with its undoubted versatility – but not enough for the Argentines to sign a cheque. That honour eventually went to Dassault-Breguet and their Super Etendard.

The *Veinticinco de Mayo* was commissioned by the Argentine Navy on 12 March 1969 and since then several further refits have taken place. Most importantly, her flight deck area was increased in 1980, but by the beginning of 1982 a new steam catapult on order from Britain had yet to be delivered. The carrier's existing catapult gear is incapable of launching a Super Etendard at maximum gross weight. Various electronic updates (notably computer-based datalink facilities between the carrier and her attendant Type 42 destroyers) have been incorporated. No Super Etendards were embarked during the invasion of the Falkland Islands (Malvinas) on 2 April 1982, or during the abortive naval operation mounted against the British Task Force in early May, which collapsed following the sinking of the aged cruiser *General Belgrano* by HMS *Conqueror*, a nuclear-powered fleet submarine.

Two days after the sinking of the *General Belgrano*, the British Task Force was still ploughing its way south and was now north of the Falklands, within the operational area and the extreme range of land-based Argentinian strike aircraft.

About 20 miles (32 km) ahead of the flagship HMS *Hermes* was HMS *Sheffield*, a 3,500-ton Type 42 destroyer armed with Sea Dart long-range air-defence missiles. As well as providing air defence of the fleet, *Sheffield* was to act as radar picket, using her Type 966 masthead 'bedstead' radar to detect any hostile ships or air attacks before they threatened the main fleet.

Just before noon on 4 May 1982, *Sheffield* was at 'Defence Stations', the second state of combat readiness, giving the crew a break from the close-up discomforts of 'Action Stations'. In the ship's galley the cooks were preparing to serve lunch. *Sheffield*'s Captain, James 'Sam' Salt, was on the bridge while a signal was sent by satellite direct to RN Fleet HQ in north-west London. The Type 966 air warning radar was temporarily shut down so as not to interfere with the transmission, but meanwhile

Seen under the starboard wing of this 11
Flotille Super Etendard is the weapon that
has given the Super Etendard its notoriety
— the Aérospatiale AM.39 Exocet anti-ship
missile.

Hermes was providing a radar picture via the tactical data link.

Then from *Sheffield*'s Operations Room came the information that three aircraft targets had been identified but had been seen to turn away. It was assumed they were Mirage IIIs probing the Task Force's defences and had declined to attack.

The assumption was tragically wrong. Suddenly the electronic support warning equipment (ESM) began to flash a warning that a radar had locked on to the ship. Again there was incomprehension as to whether it was hostile, as the computer's 'threat library' was only programmed to identify the electronic signatures of Soviet missiles as being dangerous. As the Principal Warfare Officer realised what in fact was happening, there was barely time to shout, 'Take cover'.

On the bridge Captain Salt himself saw the glow of a rocket motor and a plume of smoke. In his own account there were only four or five seconds before a massive explosion rocked the ship.

An AM.39 Exocet missile launched by a Super Etendard had ripped into the destroyer's starboard side at the level of No. 2 deck. The warhead had not exploded but the unburnt fuel and the heat of the impact had already started fires that spread through companion ways and cable runs, flashing alight the main fuel tanks and sending clouds of toxic smoke through the ship, overwhelming attempts to fight the blaze.

After five hours, and now with parts of the ship's plating glowing white-hot, the order was given to abandon ship.

What had in fact happened?

Wreathed in smoke, the Type 42 destroyer *Sheffield* seems relatively unscathed after a hit by an Exocet missile, whose warhead may well have failed to detonate.

British Intelligence knew that the Aviacion Naval Argentina had received up to eight Super Etendards armed with AM.39 Exocets and had pilots and technicians trained to fly them. In November 1981 Dassault had sent a nine-man team to Argentina to oversee the introduction of the Super Etendards, along with Aérospatiale technicians to handle the Exocet end. In April 1982 they were still there — and no-one had told them to come home. While the French government was enforcing the EEC embargo and making Mirage fighters available for Harrier pilots to engage in air-to-air combat exercises, the technical team in Argentina apparently

The first Super Etendard for Argentina taxis out for a sortie. It is seen in the markings of the 2ª Escuadrilla Aeronaval de Ataque.

worked on and repaired three of the five available launch systems which were malfunctioning.

With only eight Super Etendards available and perhaps as few as five missiles, Argentine plans for the use of these vital assets were critical. With Falklands waters now stiff with targets, the Argentine Navy's surface fleet was bottled up by British nuclear-powered fleet submarines and the carrier *Veinticinco de Mayo* could not come out even if she wanted to.

Initial planning, apparently, was for an air attack by two Super Etendards operating from the airfield at Port Stanley itself. After Operation 'Black Buck', the Vulcan raid of 1 May, and the

much more effective Harrier raids and naval bombardment thereafter, the island base was judged to be too vulnerable to risk the vital Super Etendards.

Denied a forward operating base, the 2ª Escuadrilla de Ataque was obliged to plan a mission against the Task Force by flying at extreme range from Rio Gallegos at the southern tip of the mainland. However, the Super Etendard's attack radius is a modest 400 miles (640 km) armed with an AM.39 and with maximum internal fuel load. The attack would therefore need inflight refuelling and here the Super Etendard's 'buddy pack' system would prove crucial.

By Monday 3 May, three hand-picked pilots were chosen to fly the mission. Faulty firing circuits had been detected and rectified and the complex electronic interfaces set up and aligned. At

about 10.45 on the morning of 4 May the three Super Etendards set off from Rio Gallegos, some 470 miles (756 km) from the Falklands.

Little over half an hour later, the three aircraft were within radar range of the Task Force. There is enough circumstantial evidence to suggest that the three aircraft had the approximate location of their targets (presumably the vital carriers *Hermes* and *Invincible*) already programmed into the ETNA inertial navigation system, based on intelligence derived from a submarine sighting or from a high-flying maritime patrol aircraft (such as a Lockheed SP-2H Neptune) tracking the Task Force on radar. This theory rests on the fact that the flagship *Hermes* picked up a high-level contact before the attack on *Sheffield*. There is, however,

49

another explanation for this contact.

It is more likely to have been one of the Super Etendards themselves, briefly 'popping up' above the radar horizon to take a look with its own Agave attack radar. In this supposition, the strike force formed up soon after take-off and climbed to medium altitude to conserve fuel. As they came within radar range of the Task Force, two aircraft armed with a single AM.39 each topped-up with fuel from the centre-line 'buddy pack' of the third Super Etendard. Now the formation descended to low level, to come in under the Task Force's radar, while the third aircraft climbed and lost altitude at short intervals, turning on its radar to get the target's range and bearing. It is known from Argentinian reports that the pilot saw two blips on the Agave, one large and one small, presumably *Sheffield* with *Hermes* twenty miles behind. The ETNA INS meanwhile handled the navigation, projecting steering commands on to the head-up display.

The aircraft would be in battle formation by now, strung out about two miles apart from the wingman a half mile behind the leader. The target coordinates from the pop-up Agave radar reconnaissance aircraft are communicated by a secure data link and fed into the fire-control systems. When the ETNA estimates the range at about 27 miles (45 km), the pilots pull up slightly, to give the Exocet more room for release, and the missiles are fired.

Each Exocet had to be energised before launch. The magnetron in the active radar nose needs a minute to warm up and the missile's own INS gyros need a further 36 seconds to be spun and aligned.

The Exocet has a two-part guidance system. It has its own autonomous inertial navigation system which is programmed before launch. Because, like the Super Etendard's INS and indeed the carrier that launches the aircraft, the missile automatically 'knows' where it is starting from, it can be given a set of co-ordinates and fly off in that direction without error and without any command link. It is electronically silent until its own short range homing head switches on, some five or six miles from the target. Now the missile is electronically 'live', hunting for its target by sending out electromagnetic energy and commanding itself to fly towards the biggest source of radar reflection. It is only in this mode that the missile can be thwarted electronically, by firing clouds of 'chaff' — that is, strips of aluminium foil — to present the missile with a phantom target. An onboard radio altimeter keeps the missile skimming at just above wave height with a cruising speed of Mach 0.93. It is virtually impossible to shoot down and its 364-lb (500-kg) hexolite warhead is devastating (although, as seen, the warhead

Another victim of the Exocet in the Falklands campaign was the container ship *Atlantic Conveyor*, seen here with one of the BAe Sea Harrier FRS.Mk 1 fighters it was taking to the Falklands.

on the missile that struck *Sheffield* did not explode).

With the Exocets flying under their own power and under their own autonomous inertial navigation, the Super Etendards broke off, jettisoned their drop tanks, and turned away. This is what *Sheffield* interpreted as breaking-off the action. In fact two missiles were streaking towards the ship at just below the speed of sound. Even when the Exocet went 'active' and switched on its own homing head, the *Sheffield*'s ESM computer was not programmed to recognise the threat. The destroyer had five seconds left to live.

There is however a report of a third Exocet fired at the Task Force some 25 minutes after the attack on *Sheffield*. The frigate *Yarmouth* reported sighting this missile and then fired her Corvus chaff-launchers, apparently deflecting it. Observers aboard *Alacrity* thought they saw it fall in the sea.

On 24 May the Argentine Naval Air Force used the Super Etendards again in another attempt to sink the flagship *Hermes*. Two missiles were fired and the flagship reacted by firing clouds of chaff to defeat the Exocet's homing head. Altering course to centre on the new radar target, the missiles missed

Swept by fire after the explosion of an Exocet anti-ship missile, the container ship *Atlantic Conveyor* was in fact hit by two missiles, one of which failed to detonate.

Hermes but then picked up the large container ship *Atlantic Conveyor*, packed with vital war stores and RAF Chinook heavy-lift helicopters. Two missiles struck, apparently both in the same place, but again only one exploded. The ship went ablaze and sank and three seamen and the master, Captain North, were lost in the icy waters of Falkland Sound. They were the air-launched Exocet's last victims.

Operational Assessment

Because they caused the first serious British setback of the war with the gutting of HMS *Sheffield*, the Super Etendard and the AM.39 Exocet had a tremendous public impact and gained instant notoriety. Because the missile was launched at long range and the Super Etendard pilots were not exposed to defensive fire or air-to-air combat, the method of attack had a kind of cold terror about it. This was in contrast to the Argentine Air Force and other Naval air force attacks using Skyhawks and Mirages, armed with iron bombs, coming right into the action in Falkland Channel, or even using trainer aircraft such as the Aermacchi MB 339, which sank the frigate *Ardent* with unguided ground-attack rockets. These attacks were made in the teeth of defence by naval and land based Rapier SAMs and the deadly air cover provided by Sidewinder AIM-9L-armed Sea Harriers. In all, 21 Mirage/Daggers and 13 Skyhawks were shot down. Not one Super Etendard saw action although there were reports that their mainland bases had possibly been the targets for SAS operations.

As we have seen, the success of the Super Etendard/AM.39 combination was due in part to luck, inexperience and simple mistakes. In fact two missiles failed to explode, although their impact was enough to start fires which overwhelmed their victims.

The success was unqualified, however, as far as the aircraft's export potential is concerned. In spite of the production line being shut down, Iraq wants the system for its continuing struggle with Iran, after success with Exocet-armed Super Frelon helicopters. Libya has expressed strong interest, smarting from encounters with the US Sixth Fleet in the Gulf of Sirte.

The Super Etendard carrier-based strike fighter has few rivals in its class. The US Navy carrier aircraft are very largely configured for fleet air defence and air-to-ground strike warfare. US navy aircraft are much heavier, costlier and more complex than the relatively simple transonic Super Etendard. The Etendard IVM's Royal Navy counterpart, the Hawker Siddeley Buccaneer, is still being run-on in the maritime strike role (its carriers long since gone to the scrap yard) armed with the BAe Sea Eagle Missile to replace Martel missiles, in service since the late '60s. The 100-km range Sea Eagle anti-ship missile will also arm Tornado and Sea Harrier aircraft.

The German Kormoran air-to-surface anti-ship missile, which has a similar guidance system to the AM.39 Exocet, arms West German Navy Tornados and has been ordered for Italian Tornados. The Tornado is of course a land-based aircraft with Mach 2 performance.

The US Navy put the air-launched Harpoon anti-ship missile into service in 1977 and it arms a range of aircraft including P-3 Orions, S-3 Viking ASW aircraft and attack types such as the A-6 and A-7. The Grumman A-6 Intruder, itself conceived at the same time as the Etendard IVM as a carrier-based nuclear strike aircraft, is still in production 20 years on and became operational with Harpoon in 1981.

The Super Etendard has a land-based rival closer to home in the Jaguar International, the export version of the Anglo-French Jaguar strike-trainer. One option is an Agave radar nose and AM.39 Exocet or Kormoran anti-shipping missiles, but so far none have been delivered in this configuration. With the right fit of avionics, Mirage III aircraft are also capable of operating anti-shipping missiles.

In fact virtually any modern combat aircraft, including helicopters or transport aircraft, is capable of operating as a platform for modern target acquisition, weapons-aiming avionics and for sophisticated anti-shipping missiles capable of inflicting devastating damage at long range. While Argentine Super Etendards were flying anti-shipping missile missions with Exocet, RAF Nimrods and even Vulcan bombers were armed with Harpoon missiles in case the Argentine navy should present suitable surface targets. In fact the British air-launched missile success story was the helicopter-launched Sea Skua missile, designed for use against small, fast-moving surface targets. Seven rounds were launched and all struck their targets and detonated. Thus the air-surface missile warfare in the Falklands fighting was not just all one-way.

The Future

As discussed earlier, French naval planners abandoned the *PA 75* nuclear-powered VTOL carrier project in 1980 and went instead for two nuclear-powered CTOL carriers to enter service in the 1990s. Meanwhile *Clemenceau* underwent a refit in 1978 and *Foch* had a similar refit from July 1980 to July 1981. Principal modifications were the installation of new electronic counter-measures (ECM), the SENIT 2 tactical data automation system and, for Super Etendard operations, inertial navigation system interfaces and magazines for AM.39 Exocets and AN-52 tactical nuclear weapons.

On the current plans, the first nuclear-powered carrier (probably called *Bretagne*) will replace *Foch* in 1990 and the second (probably called *Provence*) will enter service some years later.

By then the Super Etendard fleet will be halfway through its useful service life. It is planned however that the first carrier should embark Super Etendards but that these should be given up on the mid-life refit and embark, along with the second carrier, another type of aircraft. Significantly, perhaps, the new carrier's catapults will be 250 ft (77 m) long, compared to the current 165 ft (50 m) — enough

to handle the new generation of US carrier aircraft such as the F-18 strike fighter. However, more likely is a home-grown French design effort, possibly a supersonic STOVL (short take off vertical landing) aircraft. This would allow the second carrier to be fitted with a 'ski-jump' and delete the catapults, although such an advanced technology programme could well fall victim to the Aéronavale's old problem: small production runs and high unit costs.

France's main carrier strike aircraft is the Super Etendard, seen here in the form of the first production article.

Specifications

Dassault Etendard II

Type: lightweight strike fighter prototype

Accommodation: pilot only

Armament: four 20-mm Hispano-Suiza
cannon, mounted as pairs in the
lower edges of the inlet lips

Powerplant: two Turboméca Gabizo turbojets,
each rated at 2,420-lb (1,015-kg)
thrust

Performance:
maximum speed
cruising speed
initial climb rate
service ceiling
range
Weights:
empty equipped   7,937 lb (3,600 kg)
normal take-off   11,905 lb (5,400 kg)
maximum take-off
Dimensions:
span   25 ft 4¾ in (7.74 m)
length   37 ft 2 in (11.40 m)
height
wing area   227.13 sq ft (21.10 m²)

Dassault Etendard IV

Type: lightweight tactical fighter
prototype

Accommodation: pilot only

Armament: two 30-mm DEFA cannon,
mounted as single weapons in
the lower edges of the inlet lips

Powerplant: one SNECMA Atar 101E-4
turbojet, rated at 7,496-lb
(3,400-kg) thrust

Performance:
maximum speed   683 mph (1,100 km/h) at sea
level
cruising speed
initial climb rate
service ceiling
range
Weights:
empty equipped   about 11,023 lb (5,000 kg)
normal take-off   15,873 lb (7,200 kg)
maximum take-off
Dimensions:
span   31 ft 3½ in (9.54 m)
length   47 ft 3 in (14.40 m)
height   13 ft 7⅓ in (4.15 m)
wing area   270.1 sq ft (25.10 m²)

Dassault Etendard VI

Type: lightweight tactical fighter
prototype

Accommodation: pilot only

Armament: four 0.5-in (12.7-mm) Colt-
Browning machine-guns,
mounted as pairs in the lower
edges of the inlet lips

Powerplant: one Bristol Siddeley Orpheus
Bor. 3 turbojet, rated at 4,850-lb
(2,200-kg) thrust

Performance:
maximum speed
cruising speed
initial climb rate
service ceiling
range
Weights:
empty equipped   7,496 lb (3,400 kg)
normal take-off   12,125 lb (5,500 kg)
maximum take-off
Dimensions:
span   26 ft 10⅝ in (8.20 m)
length   37 ft 2 in (11.40 m)
height   11 ft 5¾ in (3.50 m)
wing area   226.04 sq ft (21.00 m²)

Dassault Etendard IVM

Type: shipboard interceptor and
tactical strike fighter

Accommodation: pilot only, seated on a Martin-
Baker ejector seat

Armament: two 30-mm DEFA cannon,
mounted as single weapons in
the lower edges of the inlet lips,
plus up to 3,307 lb (1,500 kg)
of weapons on four underwing
hardpoints; typical loads are two
AIM-9 Sidewinder AAMs, or
two AS.30 ASMs, or two
1,000-lb (454-kg) and two
500-lb (227-kg) bombs

Powerplant: one SNECMA Atar 08B turbojet,
rated at 9,700-lb (4,400-kg)
thrust

Performance:
maximum speed   673 mph (1,093 km/h) or Mach
1.02 at 36,090 ft (11,000 m)
and 683 mph (1,100 km/h) or
Mach 0.9 at sea level
initial climb rate   19,685 ft (6,000 m) per minute
service ceiling
range   435-mile (700-km) radius on a
high-altitude interception
mission
Weights:
empty equipped   13,503 lb (6,125 kg)
normal take-off   18,011 lb (8,170 kg)
maximum take-off   22,652 lb (10,275 kg)
Dimensions:
span   31 ft 6 in (9.60 m)
length   47 ft 3 in (14.40 m)
height   14 ft 2 in (4.30 m)
wing area   312.16 sq ft (29.00 m²)

Dassault-Breguet Super Etendard

Type: shipboard interceptor and
tactical strike fighter

Accommodation: pilot only, seated on a Martin-
Baker ejector seat

Armament: two 30-mm DEFA cannon,
mounted as single weapons in
the lower edges of the inlet lips,
plus up to 4,630 lb (2,100 kg)
on a double underfuselage and
four underwing hardpoints;
typical loads are two Matra 550
Magic AAMs, or six 551-lb
(250-kg) bombs, or four 882-lb
(400-kg) bombs, or four 18-tube
rocket-launchers, or one
AM.39 Exocet anti-ship missile,
or one AN-52 nuclear bomb

Powerplant: one SNECMA Atar 08K-50
turbojet, rated at 11,023-lb
(5,000-kg) thrust

Performance:
maximum speed   673 mph (1,093 km/h) or Mach
1.02 at 36,090 ft (11,000 m)
and 733 mph (1,180 km/h) or
Mach 0.96 at sea level
initial climb rate   19,685 ft (6,000 m) per minute
service ceiling   44,950 ft (13,700 m)
range   530-mile (850-km) hi-lo-hi
radius with one AM.39 and
external tank
Weights:
empty equipped   14,330 lb (6,500 kg)
normal take-off   20,833 lb (9,450 kg)
maximum take-off   26,455 lb (12,000 kg)
Dimensions:
span   31 ft 6 in (9.60 m)
length   46 ft 11½ in (14.31 m)
height   12 ft 8 in (3.86 m)
wing area   305.7 sq ft (28.40 m²)

Etendard series production

Etendard II: three ordered, but only one
completed.
Etendard IV: one only.
Etendard VI: one only.
Etendard IVM: one prototype, six pre-
production aircraft (construction
numbers 01–06) and 61 production
aircraft (construction numbers 1–69).
Etendard IVP: one pre-production aircraft
(construction number 07) and 21
production aircraft (construction
numbers 101–121).
Super Etendard: three prototypes (all
converted Etendard IVM aircraft), plus
71 production aircraft for France (construction numbers 1–71), 14 production
aircraft for Argentina (serial numbers
0751–0760 and 0771–0774, coded
from 3–A–201 to 3–A–214) and
possibly six production aircraft for Iraq.

Dassault-Breguet Super Etendard technical description

Type: carrier- and land-based all-weather transonic strike fighter and interceptor.

Wings: the basic configuration is that of a cantilever mid-wing monoplane, with a quarter-chord sweep of 45°, anhedral of 3° 30' and thickness/chord ratio declining from 6 per cent at the roots to 5 per cent at the tips; an all-metal two-spar torsion box structure is used, with a stressed-skin all-metal covering of machined panels with integral stiffeners; the portions of the wings outboard of the inset ailerons fold upwards for carrier stowage; high-lift devices comprise double-slotted flaps on the inboard section of each trailing edge, and hydraulically powered drooping leading edges with extended-chord dogtooth on the outer portion; control is vested in two inset ailerons, hydraulically operated by irreversible dual-circuit Dassault actuators with artificial 'feel', and there is a spoiler on the upper surface of each wing ahead of the ailerons.

Fuselage: all-metal semi-monocoque structure waisted in accordance with the area rule, and fitted with twin perforated airbrakes, one located on each side of the underside of the centre fuselage.

Tail unit: this is a cantilever all-metal structure, the horizontal tail located halfway up the vertical surfaces, all of which are swept; the tailplane is all-moving, and like the rudder is powered by irreversible dual-circuit Dassault hydraulic actuators with artificial 'feel'; the tailplane also has electric pitch trim.

Landing gear: this is of the retractable tricycle type, with a single wheel on each unit, and made by Messier-Hispano-Bugatti; the nosewheel retracts rearward into the lower fuselage, and the main units inwards into the undersurfaces of the wings and the lower fuselage; the nosewheel has a 490 x 155-9 tyre, and each of the mainwheels a 30 x 7.7-16 tyre; all oleo-pneumatic shock-absorbers and disc brakes are by Messier-Hispano-Bugatti; a braking parachute is stowed in a fairing at the trailing-edge junction of the horizontal and vertical tail surfaces, and a V-shape arrester hook is fitted to the underside of the rear fuselage.

Powerplant and fuel system: one 11,023-lb (5,000-kg) thrust SNECMA Atar 08K-50 turbojet located in the central fuselage, with lateral inlets alongside the cockpit and the nozzle under the tail surfaces; fuel is fed to the engine from integral wing tanks and rubber fuselage tanks with a combined capacity of 719 Imp gal (3,270 litres); external fuel provisions are for one 132-Imp gal (600-litre) drop-tank under the fuselage, or two 132-Imp gal (600-litre) drop-tanks on the inner pair of underwing hardpoints, or two 242-Imp gal (1,100-litre) drop-tanks on the inner pair of underwing hardpoints; inflight-refuelling capability is provided by a retractable probe housed in a fairing forward of the windscreen; the centreline hardpoint can also accommodate a Douglas-designed 'buddy' refuelling pod so that the Super Etendard can refuel other Super Etendards.

Accommodation: pilot only, seated on a Hispano-built Martin-Baker SEMBB CM4A lightweight ejector seat in the armoured, pressurised and air-conditioned cockpit.

Electronics and operational equipment: the Super Etendard's operational capability is centred on the Thomson-CSF/ESD Agave lightweight radar, which provides the pilot with search, track, designation, navigation and telemetry information via a Thomson-CSF VE-120 head-up display and Crouzet Type 97 navigation display, which also receives input from the Sagem-Kearfott ETNA inertial navigation system and the Type 66 air-data computer; provision is made under the fuselage for a reconnaissance pod.

Armament: this comprises a pair of 30-mm DEFA cannon with 125 rounds per gun (one cannon in the lower edge of each inlet lip), and provision for an external load of up to 4,360 lb (2,100 kg) on one underfuselage and four underwing hardpoints; the fuselage hardpoint is rated at 1,323 lb (600 kg), each of the inner underwing hardpoints at 2,425 lb (1,100 kg) and each of the outer underwing hardpoints at 992 lb (450 kg); typical loads are two Matra 550 Magic dog-fighting air-to-air missiles, or six 551-lb (250-kg) free-fall or retarded bombs, or four 882-lb (400-kg) free-fall or retarded bombs, or four LR150 rocket-launcher pods each with 18 68-mm (2.68-in) rockets, or (in specially fitted aircraft) one AM.39 Exocet anti-ship missile under the starboard wing and balanced by a 242-Imp gal (1,100-litre) drop-tank under the port wing, or (in French aircraft only) one AN-52 free-fall nuclear bomb.

Systems: all systems are hydraulically powered by duplicated circuits.

Acknowledgments

We would particularly like to thank Monsieur A. Segura of Avions Marcel Dassault-Breguet Aviation for his invaluable help with the pictures for this publication.

Picture research was through Military Archive and Research Services, Braceborough, Lincolnshire, and unless otherwise indicated below all material was supplied by Dassault.
Aérospatiale: pp. 4–5, 19 (centre), 46–47.
Blitz: pp. 6–7.
Crown Copyright (Fleet Photographic Unit: pp. 48, 50–51.
GIFAS: pp. 36, 38–39.
Military Archive and Research Services: p. 19 (top).
SIRPA (Marine Nationale): pp. 19 (bottom), 26 (bottom), 27, 28–29, 31, 32–33, 35, 40–41, 42 (top and bottom), 44 (top and centre), 52–53.
SNECMA: pp. 9, 13, 18.
Thomson-CSF: pp. 32, 33.